ON THE ROAD

CAN YOU SEE WHAT I SEE?
ON THE ROAD

by Walter Wick

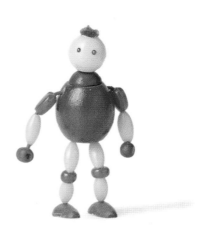

SCHOLASTIC INC.

New York   Toronto   London   Auckland   Sydney   Mexico City
New Delhi   Hong Kong   Buenos Aires

Published by Scholastic Inc.

SCHOLASTIC, CARTWHEEL BOOKS, and

associated logos are trademarks and/or

registered trademarks of Scholastic Inc.

Images on pages 26-27 and 32-33 © 2008 are new to

this edition.

"Bump, Bump, Bump!" and "Domino Effect" from

Can You See What I See? © 2002 by Walter Wick;

"Thirteen O'clock," "Rocket Motors," "Sky High," and

"Bedtime" from *Can You See What I See? Dream

Machine* © 2003 by Walter Wick; "Traffic Jam" from

Can You See What I See? Cool Collections © 2004

by Walter Wick; "Hansel and Gretel," "Puss in Boots,"

and "Cinderella" from *Can You See What I See?

Once Upon a Time* © 2006 by Walter Wick.

ISBN-13: 978-0-545-04709-8

ISBN-10: 0-545-04709-9

10 9 8 7 6 5 4 3 2 1   08 09 10 11 12/0

Printed in Singapore 46

This edition first printing, January 2008

Book Design by Walter Wick and David Saylor

Acknowledgments:

Set construction and custom models were built in my studio with the help of two staff members and several freelance artists. I would like to extend my grateful appreciation and thanks to my longtime staff members Daniel Helt and Kim Wildey, and freelance artists Michael Lokensgaard, Bruce Morozko, Randy Gilman, Mike Galvin, and Lynne Steincamp for their talent, dedication, and many artistic contributions to the pictures in *On the Road*.

CONTENTS

Can you see
what I see?
A popped-up hood,
an open door,
a race car
with the number 4,
a checkered flag,
a truck for mail,
a traffic cone,
a car for sale,
a motorbike,
a plane, a plow,
a horse's head,
3 ducks, a cow!

Can you see
what I see?
5 puzzle pieces,
a ruler, a queen,
a hand that points
to number 13,
6 pencils, a cow,
a bunny, 4 birds,
a catchy slogan
with 2 rhyming words,
a girl with a bow,
a hand in a pocket,
a spoon on a plate,
a man in a rocket!

Can you see
what I see?
A wolf that howls,
a bear that's sweet,
a broom, a bat,
2 worms to eat,
an owl, an acorn,
an ax, a nail,
a deer, a dove,
a shovel, a snail,
a red raspberry,
a rolling pin,
a witch who beckons,
"Come in, come in!"

Can you see
what I see?
A hot dog, a soda,
fries on the side,
a truck at the start
of a long bumpy ride,
9 yellow flags,
3 arrows, a king,
a wagon, a web,
an ocean, a spring,
2 tiger paws,
5 camel humps —
get the EGGS
to the EXIT
crossing only
3 bumps!

Can you see
what I see?
A man in a helmet,
a man in a hat,
a watering can,
a curious cat,
a candle,
3 matches,
a blue bird, a bell,
a pencil, a wrench,
2 thimbles, a shell,
the eye of a needle,
a mouse that is red,
a car in for service,
DREAM CITY ahead!

Can you see
what I see?
5 bowling pins,
a pencil,
a nail,
2 black hats,
a lion's tail,
a tennis racket,
a lazy frog,
2 cymbals,
3 thimbles,
an obedient dog,
a domino cart,
a rolling ball —
the only clown
about to fall!

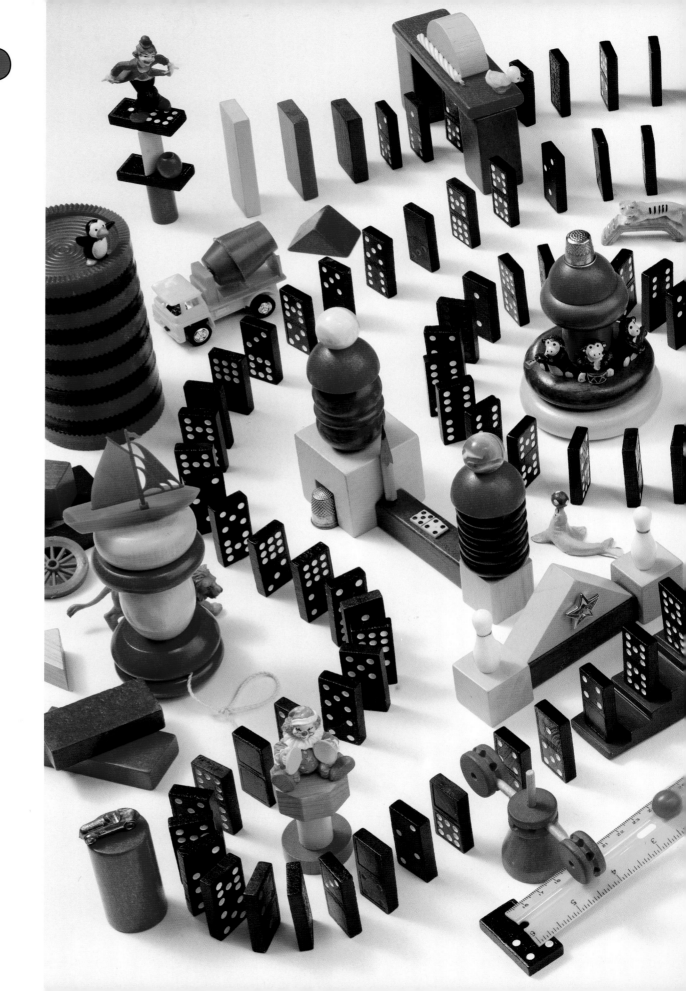

Can you see
what I see?
A fox, 4 rabbits,
a pinecone, a pear,
a torch, a trumpet,
an archer, a bear,
7 black birds,
a windmill, a well,
a dragon, a deer,
a basket, a bell,
the marquis's carriage,
a white-plumed hat,
an ogre's frown,
and one clever cat!

Can you see
what I see?
A silver phone,
a yellow funnel,
a red jet-car
inside a tunnel,
a shuttlecock,
a filling station,
a billboard
for a space vacation,
the planet Earth,
a fish, red thread,
a saltshaker laser
on a robot head!

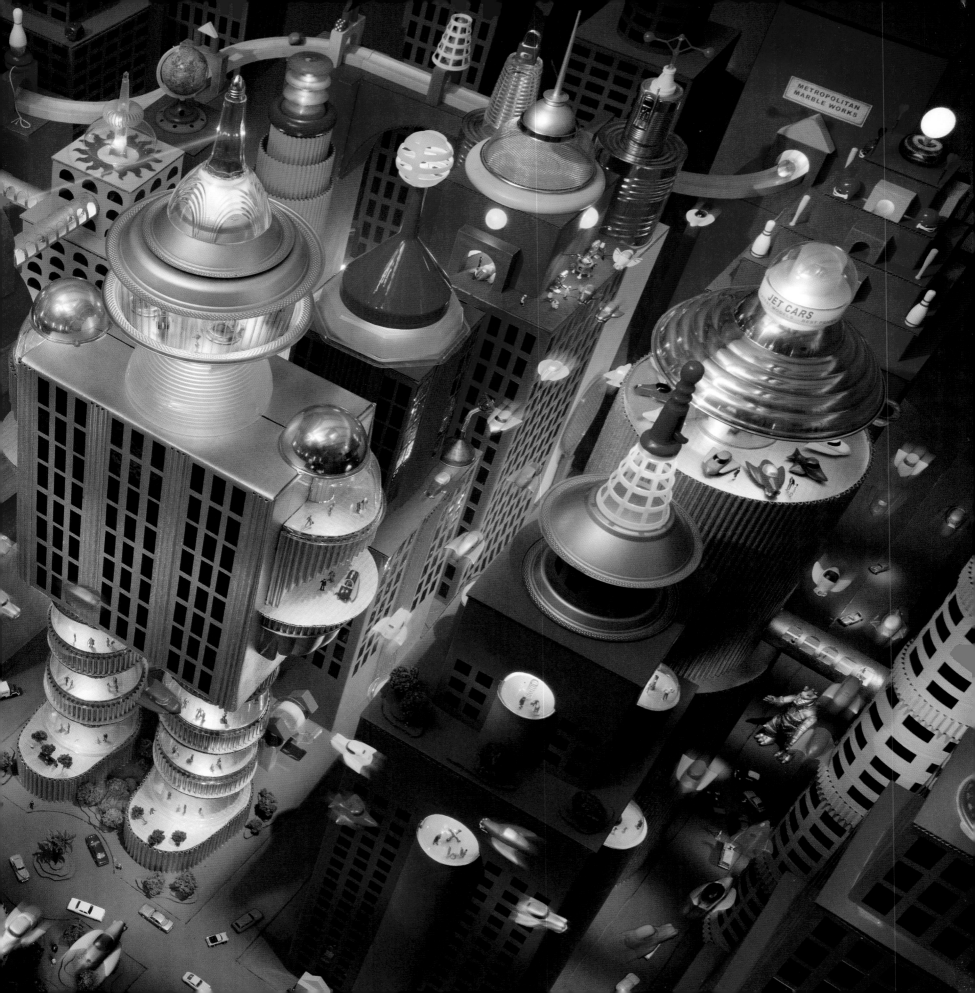

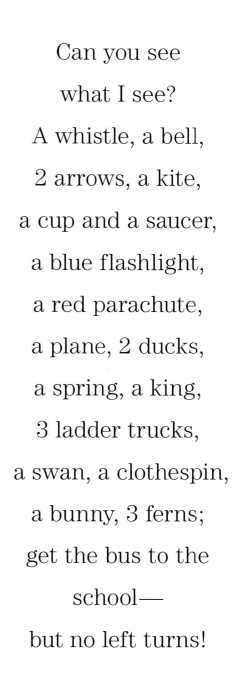

Can you see
what I see?
A whistle, a bell,
2 arrows, a kite,
a cup and a saucer,
a blue flashlight,
a red parachute,
a plane, 2 ducks,
a spring, a king,
3 ladder trucks,
a swan, a clothespin,
a bunny, 3 ferns;
get the bus to the
school—
but no left turns!

Can you see
what I see?
A broken heart,
a knight, a moon,
an instrument
that plays a tune,
a pumpkin coach,
an owl, a hare,
a butterfly,
a teddy bear,
a rat in a hat,
a prince in blue,
and Cinderella's
slipper, too!

Can you see
what I see?
5 cards, a bike,
3 soccer balls,
a spotted owl,
striped overalls,
an elephant,
a dog asleep,
a dinosaur tail,
7 white sheep,
a yo-yo, a boat,
a can, a jar,
a lightning bolt
on a little red car!

Can you see
what I see?
A robot building,
a gingerbread house,
a big blue funnel,
a trap for a mouse,
a baseball bat,
3 ladders, a stool,
a robot monster,
a DINER, a SCHOOL,
a sliver of moon,
a rabbit that's green,
and an artist at work
behind the scenes!

This special Scholastic Book Fair edition, *Can You See What I See? On the Road,* brings together pictures and rhymes from previous titles in the Can You See What I See? series that celebrate the spirit of movement, travel, and adventure. In addition there are two previously unpublished picture puzzles: "No Left Turns" features a puzzle-within-a-puzzle maze, and "Behind the Scenes" shows me at work in my studio as well as close-up details of other photographs in the book.

I am often asked: "How do you make your pictures?"; "How big are your sets?"; "How long does it take you to make a book?"; and "Where do you get all that stuff?" I like to think of "Behind the Scenes" as a field trip to my studio and an opportunity for you to learn the answers to those questions.

You may want to take some time to compare the fifteen pictures in "Behind the Scenes" with the other eleven photographs in this book.

The picture in the lower left corner shows my storage bins for *Dream Machine*. In those bins, toys are mixed in with ordinary household items—my stock in trade. Many of the items are from my collection, which has grown over many years. I purchased other items at dollar stores, party stores, and discount outlets. There are six other behind-the-scene pictures from *Dream Machine*. Can you find them? Notice the ordinary materials used to make buildings, how crowded the studio looks, and how big the sets look when I am in the picture. It took me and my helpers three months to make "Sky High" (pages 24–25) and many more months to complete the pictures in *Dream Machine*.

"Puss in Boots" and "Cinderella" from *Once Upon a Time* each took several weeks to construct. The castles were made out of polyurethane foam—somewhat like Styrofoam but much harder, so that it can be carved like wood. Look for the castle in "Cinderella." Only the front of the castle was built because that's all that was needed for the picture. The castle for "Puss and Boots" was put on top of a tall hill (also made of foam) to create a dramatic perspective. The grass and trees are the type used for model railroads and were purchased at a hobby shop.

On the Road features three maze puzzles ("Bump, Bump, Bump!"; "Domino Effect"; and "No Left Turns") that provide a twist on the theme of travel as well as an extra challenge. I made these with toys from my collection— dominoes, building blocks, and toy cars. Such pictures take less time to build since there is little model–making involved. But blending a challenging maze with a search-and-find puzzle can be tricky and can extend what would be about a four- or five-day project into three weeks.

Finally, you can see me at work on "Traffic Jam" from *Cool Collections*. While the sight of so many cars and trucks in one picture might suggest otherwise, this picture was one of the easiest for me to photograph. Using cars from my collection (nearly all of them), I arranged them on a white tabletop, using a yardstick to keep them in alignment. Total build time? About three days.

And one more question that I don't want to forget: "What comes first, the pictures or the rhymes?" I believe that the best way to make picture puzzles for Can You See What I See? is to make the pictures first. As I build the sets, I am always on the lookout for clever hiding opportunities. When the picture is nearly complete I start writing the rhyme, usually starting with words that would help support the visual theme of the photograph. But I am always ready to change the rhyme at the last minute, for I am always studying the picture I have created for an unexpected play on words, a humorous touch, or a particularly clever hiding place that I could not have imagined while sitting in front of a computer!

— Walter Wick

Walter Wick is the photographer of the I Spy series of books, with more than twenty-nine million copies in print. He is author and photographer of *A Drop of Water: A Book of Science and Wonder*, which won the Boston Globe/Horn Book Award for Nonfiction, was named a Notable Children's Book by the American Library Association, and was selected as an Orbis Pictus Honor Book and a CBC/NSTA Outstanding Science Trade Book for Children. *Walter Wick's Optical Tricks*, a book of photographic illusions, was named a Best Illustrated Children's Book by the *New York Times Book Review*, was recognized as a Notable Children's Book by the American Library Association, and received many awards, including a Platinum Award from the Oppenheim Toy Portfolio, a Young Readers Award from *Scientific American*, a *Bulletin* Blue Ribbon, and a Parents' Choice Silver Honor. *Can You See What I See?*, published in 2003, appeared on the *New York Times* Bestseller List for twenty-two weeks. Other books in the Can You See What I See? series are *Dream Machine*, *Cool Collections*, *The Night Before Christmas*, and *Once Upon a Time*. Mr. Wick has invented photographic games for *GAMES* magazine and photographed covers for books and magazines, including *Newsweek*, *Discover*, and *Psychology Today*. A graduate of Paier College of Art, Mr. Wick lives in Connecticut with his wife, Linda.

More information about Walter Wick is available at www.walterwick.com.